T0065504

CAT
MEOWS 2

THE TALE OF CAT

CAT. E. GOIN

WESTBOW
PRESS®
A DIVISION OF THOMAS NELSON
& ZONDERVAN

This book is a work of non-fiction. Unless otherwise noted, the author and the publisher make no explicit guarantees as to the accuracy of the information contained in this book and in some cases, names of people and places have been altered to protect their privacy.

WestBow Press books may be ordered through booksellers or by contacting:

WestBow Press
A Division of Thomas Nelson & Zondervan
1663 Liberty Drive
Bloomington, IN 47403
www.westbowpress.com
844-714-3454

Because of the dynamic nature of the Internet, any web addresses or links contained in this book may have changed since publication and may no longer be valid. The views expressed in this work are solely those of the author and do not necessarily reflect the views of the publisher, and the publisher hereby disclaims any responsibility for them.

Any people depicted in stock imagery provided by Getty Images are models, and such images are being used for illustrative purposes only. Certain stock imagery © Getty Images.

ISBN: 978-1-6642-5858-7 (sc)
ISBN: 978-1-6642-5857-0 (e)

Library of Congress Control Number: 2022903597

Print information available on the last page.

WestBow Press rev. date: 05/02/2022

Dedicated to:

Dr. Zigmund Lebensohn

Dr. Wang

Dr. David Goldstein

This short book is also dedicated to CAT (now deceased) and her beloved POP (my beloved brother Russell I. Goin)

But I tell you a cat needs a particular name
A name that' peculiar and more dignified,
Else how can he keep his tail perpendicular
Or spread out his whiskers, or cherish his pride.

T.S. Eliot from "Old Possum's Book of Particular Cats."

Contents

Sometimes the World Misses CAT

Sometimes the world misses CAT who was Pop's friend long, long ago

Who was my friend long, long ago.

She was beautiful…gray…little paws of white

She was a lady; she did not fight.

She had long ago seen the light.

She liked to go out and visit the neighborhood…it suited her mood

At slinking around she was good.

A flick of a whisker here, a flick of a whisker there,

She apparently did not have a care and she could stare down any mouse

Who had been lingering at our house.

She liked to visit with me, she was my muse…her I never did confuse

She would watch soaps, sitting beside me on the floor as I faced the door,

Always, always wanting to leave.

CAT's Meows...no. 1

CAT! I am!

Siblings! None

I...the only one!

To gain my trust you must...

Oh, yes, I recall...

When I was small...

Happy child!

      Never whimpered...

      Never simpered...

      Nor did I cry...

Me! Most superior

Outdoors and in the interior...

      Yes indeedy...most superior!

Rattlesnake, he is afraid because

I am quick and my fangs are sharp

      As they tear the rattler apart!

Rain, sleet, hail

      It do fall!

I scamper into the dining hall...

Where I indulge...

      Kibbles and meat

      An occasional tidbit

Of a sweet!

Frosting...a delicacy infrequently!

Pop so contrary...not ordinary!

No ordinary cat myself...so cool!

CAT's Meows...no. 2

Flee, flee from me...me
Horrible, horrible, nasty fleas!
Dig into my dainty hide
There, unless Pop uses flea powder, they will abide!
    Chewing my gorgeous side!
    Chewing my dainty hide!

Worse and worse...ticks...a hideous curse
Fatten by drinking my blood!
    Glob, glob, glob!

Flee! Flee! From Me! Me!
Horrible, horrible ticks and fleas!

CAT's Meows...no. 3

I bite/bit the mouse mighty hard
We were scampering across the yard!
     I grabbed his tail
     He flailed about, did holler and shout
He tried to jump away from me
He did not get free!

I worry that Pop
Does not get enough to eat!
I was bringing him some meat!

Moral is...
     Chasing mice is my biz...
As is chasing a lizard
     So as I can eat his gizzard!

CAT's Meows...no. 4

Pop wants to go on a camping trip

He prefers a canoe

I prefers a ship!

Running water all thru' my fur

Shivers convulse Me!

I say "brrr."

He loads canoe...supplies

Dinner cooking

　　　　While I dries!

A bear my appear

Also raccoons or deer!

Rufus, a remarkable dog

Sits on his seat

Like a bump on a log.

AT's Meows...no. 5

Sittin' in the sun!

Days' work never done!

Sittin' in the sun!

Breeze quietly blows, blows

Pop mows, flowers grows...

Peaceful, peaceful on the deck...

Sun goes down....

A speck of dust floatin'

      Here

      There

Nary a thought, nary a care

Floatin' here, floatin' there!

AT's Meows...no. 6

Oh, dearest mousie
Headin' for your hole…
      I prefer a rabbit
      Perhaps a mole.
Into which I can sink my teeth
Mighty, mighty tasty!
My belief!

To your hole in the living room
You are headed!
ZOOM! ZOOM! ZOOM!

I, too, am through
Playin' with you!
I prefer to sun on the deck
In the backyard!

All this activity
Has made me tired!

CAT's Purrs...no. 1

I! Splendiferous
I! Carnivorous!
I! CAT! Sat!
Deep in thought about the mouse
Caught gallivantin' about the house
      Whiskers twitchin'
      Tail flippin', tail switchin'
Through the atmosphere...
Through the air!
I hungry! That is clear!
Should I bite? I might!
It's head off or not?
I! thought!
Thought a lot!
Mousie encased in a hide of gray
Thinkin', "How do I get away?"
      Smack! Whack!
      Upside the head
      So clumsy!

Mousie will be dead!
And I will have to play with catnip instead!
"Oh, little Mousie! Don't be dead."

CAT's Purrs...no. 2

My friend! So depressed~

    She had not bothered to get dressed…

    Jeans unpressed!

    A mess!

I! Jumped upon her lap

My! Tail! Went flap, flap, flap

I! put my paws upon her breast

Even though she was not dressed

Her best!

    I! looked deep into her eyes

    She looked at my claws

    Stickin' outside my paws

    They stretched…unstretched!

I! purred my loudest

I! purred and purred

I! gently gazed! Then amazed!

She got happy again, My friend!

ℂAT's Purrs...no. 3

Tick! Tock! Tick! Tock!

Goes the existential clock!

It does put my tail in shock!

First this way and then that

As I traipse around the block

Keepin' me from getting' fat.

      Sleek, slim!

      Quite the miss

      I look into the mirror!

      I could give myself a kiss!

Oh, so pretty, so sublime

Like that clock tickin' time!

Flick goes my whiskers

In time with my tail

      Flitter and flutter

      Twist and flail!

      Whiskers and tail!

Oh, existential clock on the wall

So busy, don't fall

Oh, existential clock

Metallic, silvery gray

      Tickin' tockin'

Time speeds on its way!

      Tickin', tockin'

Night and day!
Silvery, silvery, silvery gray
Tickin', tockin'
Life speeds on its way
Indeedy!
Life speeds on its way!

"Wally", said CAT perturbed
"Pop has gone fishin' I have heard."
He has not invited me to attend
When he has to gut the fish
And de-fin them he does not wince."

"CAT, oh CAT," said Wally, Pop's pal
"CAT, you are quite a gal
You gobble up mice, birds
An occasional fish
Not even usin' your dish."

"Wally," said CAT in a much louder voice
"Leavin' me home was not a nice choice.
I will avenge myself! Believe!
Even though vengeance is hard to achieve."
Vengeance, oh glory, vengeance so gory.
I could have caught a Moray Eel...
Hear it squeal as I bit off its head
In a flash! Dead!

"Wally," said CAT
"I am starvin'! Are you carvin?
That fish for my meal? I do love you so!
My feelings I feel!

CAT requested more
Gathered her tail and slunk out the door.

Later, much later Pop arrived home
CAT wanted to call him
But couldn't use the phone.
  She was lackin' an opposable thumb
  She was thwarted
  No...no...NOT dumb!

Quietly, quietly on her pussy foots
She pounced on Pop's shoulder
  Bolder! Bolder! Bolder!
Now that she had eaten her fill
She no longer needed to go out to kill!

CAT's Purrs...no. 5

Happy! Happy!
To know my fur is best
When at rest!

My tail lies straight under the weight
Of its skin and bones
It fits within!

"Oh, Pop!" I cry
I wonder why the daisies bloom
Perfume the room
The white and yellow blooms
Pierces the glooms!"

"Pop," I say "I'll show you the way
To proceed through daily life
Unencumbered by daily strife
Which is daily abundantly rife.
You ask... have I CAT, been a wife?
Why no, you see
Matrimony doesn't agree with me.
I like to sleep and roam
Unencumbered by anyone at home.
The tomcats I have known
Color me wrong, disengage my song

I don't want to tag along
It suffices to have pleasure without measure
Tomcats inhibit me
Which way I don't want to be!

Tee Hee! Tee Hee! Tee Hee!
Dear tomcats, let me be
Tee Hee! Tee Hee! Tee Hee!

CAT's Purrs...no. 6

The evening gloom pierces the room
Pop is on his porch havin' a beer
  I sit near!
  Great, great Pop
Whom I truly love a lot!

Clouds up high in the darkening sky
Yellow/orange peeps above the edge
  Spreading a hazy glow!
  Or is it a lazy glow?
I'm just CAT! How should I know?

I love the evening glow
Sparkling as the evening wind does blow!
Glorious, glorious evening glow!

The sky darkens, the stars sparkling
  Not a care
If I was not CAT I would be a star
Spreadin' my light here and thar'
Twinkly, twinkly evening star

AT's Purrs...no. 7

The spider scampered across the rug
It has eight legs, it's not a bug!
The rug is from a Persian loom
It fills the floor, it fills the room
It lightens up the evening gloom.
> Fireflies glitter, fill the night
> With their flashin', yellow light.

I am hungry, Pop's at work
So, near the mousehole I will lurk
Huntin' for dinner is a winner
> A task I cannot shirk!

Myself, I purrs
The ceiling fan whirrs!
> Coolin' off the living space
> Coolin' off the entire place!

I find that huntin' challenges my mind
Huntin' causes me to purrs
Gently, gently as the ceiling fan whirs!

ⒸAT's Purrs...no. 8

I!! CAT!!

Sittin

      On the windowsill

Chantin' to myself

      I will not

            Will not

                  Will not

                        Kill!

Robins!

Their feathers

      Are so pretty...

Will soon be in my stomach....

      A pity...

I could not do this

      In the city!

      A pity!!!

AT's Gurrs...no. 1

OH! Disgusting Mousie!
Scamperin', scurryin' around the house
Leavin' footprints on the floor
While he is lookin' for food!

  For into his stomach to go
  Disturbin' my Zen-like flow
  So! Off I go! Pouncin' in a flash!

If I get him, he will be a gourmet dish
Better than fish!
Off I go, in a flash!

He goes hurriedly past
He will make a delicious repast!
Oh! How splendiferous! Oh, how stupendous!

  I will catch him! I will!
  I will chew him and chew him
  I certainly will!

Then I'll settle down gleefully for the night
No longer hungry, I'll put out the light!

AT's Gurrs...no. 2

I look a sight! I look a fright!
My fur is wet!
Not much sorrier can I, CAT, get
Dignity deserts me, does flee!

Please dear God who lives above
Who assures me of His love
Even when my fur is soppin' wet!
Not much sorrier can I, CAT, get
Filled with disgust, I might rust!

Rats! It's rainin', my fur is gainin'
Weight by the minute! Doggone it!
I hate wet fur...obnoxious for sure
Absolutely toxic...it makes me moan and groan!
Rats! Rain!
Leave my fur alone!

AT's Gurrs...no. 3

Sittin' in the sun is so much fun

Lazy, don't get much done

Pop wonders how I can rest so much

He's energetic, thinks nappin' is a crutch.

      He was frenetic 'til he took up with me

      He thought nappin' a waste of energy!

But now he lies on the couch

In the middle of the day

Nods off by himself, not such a grouch!

Anddddd...I, CAT, have a hunch

He'll nap again after lunch

In front of the fire, all aglow

He's as lazy as me, don't you know?

AT's Gurrs...no. 4

Sun shines down ...upon my fur! I, CAT, happy...purr!

The windowsill is the place to be

I, CAT, happy...so happy

Tee! Hee!

Sissy CAT, Prissy CAT, Hissy CAT!

Preenin' my fur upon the sill

> Wonderin'? Wonderin'? Will?
>
> Will I what? Will I how?
>
> I am so beautiful!
>
> Now! Wow!

My fur lies on my skin just right!

Not too loose, not too tight!

Fallin' on my skin just right!

I talk to Pop at breakfast

Before into his car he hops

Headin' to his place of work

I talk! It is my duty!

I must not shirk!

> I am so beautiful, I must say!
>
> Perfect in every way!

CAT's Gurrs...no. 5

I will nap! Springtime!
The sap flows into the limbs of the
Neighbor trees, bendin' and swayin'
In the afternoon breeze!
We'll raise our voices in praise of Him
Who sits on high and admires the universe
He wrought! He says to me
"You ought to take a walk! Nap later!
For at this time I was slumberin'
And dreamin' of an alligator
Who flaps his lips; and bares his teeth
Wantin' to sink them into my hide!
Alligators I can't abide!

AT's Gurrs...no. 6

CAT...sittin' on the fence

Admirin' the day, watching a bird!

Ever so intense!

 Bird! Ever so tasty in a whole -wheat pastry

 Wonderful delicacy...bird!

 CAT caught bird and took a bite!

CAT chewed to the left; CAT chewed to the right!

Not uptight!

Bird tasted just right...CAT took another bite!

Magnificent! Out of sight!

CAT sighed and took another bite!

CAT's Gurrs...no. 7

It's late! It's dark! Hark! A lark!
A speck of light from a distant star'
Helpin' me to see afar!
I patrol the grounds
Dutifully makin' the rounds
Behind each bush I look
Breakin' off a branch of a tree
Sometimes four, hardly ever more!
It's late! It's dark! Hark! A lark!

AT's Gurrs...no. 8

CAT left the house ...after dinner...a mouse!

The rock In the yard, CAT noticed, was tired!

It had had a long day, no time to play!

Surrounded by pebbles and stones

In addition to the bones CAT had chewed

And spit on the ground, near the rock she had found!

Sittin's so gray, sittin' alone

Surrounded by the remnants of CAT's dinner...

Mouse bones!

CAT's Gurrs...no. 9

Oh! Disgusting Mousie!

Scamperin'. Scurryin' around the house

Leavin' footprints on the floor

He looks for more food

For into his stomach to go!

Disturbin' my Zen-like flow...

      So, off I go!

        Pouncin' in a flash!

If I get him, he'll be a gourmet dish

Better than fish!

Off I go! In a flash!

He goes hurriedly, in a flash!

He will be a delicious repast!

Oh! How splendiferous!

Oh! How stupendous!

I will catch him! I will!

I will chew him and chew him

I certainly will!

Then I'll settle down peacefully

      For the night!

No longer hungry, I'll turn off the light!

The End...except for an excerpt from:

"Old Possum's Book of Practical Cats" by T.S. Elliot

No.1

When you notice a cat in profound meditation

The reason, I tell you, is always the same:

His mind is engaged in a rapt contemplation

Of the thought, of the thought. Of the thought of his name.

His ineffable effable

Effanineffable

Deep and inscrutable singular Name.

Printed in the United States
by Baker & Taylor Publisher Services

Printed in the United States
by Baker & Taylor Publisher Services